United States Air F

FOR KIDS

by Eric Z

All images are in the public domain unless otherwise noted.

This image or file is a work of a U.S. Air Force Airman or employee, taken or made as part of that person's official duties. As a work of the U.S. federal government, the image or file is in the public domain.

беларуская (тарашкевіца) | català | čeština | Deutsch | English | español | eesti | فارسی | suomi | italiano | 日本語 | 한국어 | македонски | മലയാളം | Plattdüütsch | Nederlands | polski | português | русский | slovenčina | српски / srpski | Türkçe | Tiếng Việt | 中文 | 中文（简体） | +/–

GET NAVY SEALS FOR KIDS
For FREE
Go to the end of this book and follow the link!

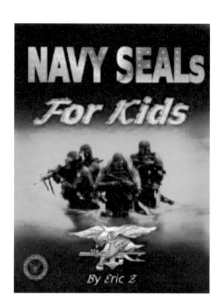

To all the kids who want to be an Air Force Pilot

Preface

Do you want to be an Air Force pilot? There are a few things you should know before you start on your journey. If you follow the advice in this book, you will be well on your way to becoming an Air Force Pilot! — and always remember, *AIM HIGH!*

Contents

Joining the Air Force

If you want to be an Air Force Pilot, <u>you must meet the requirements.</u> They don't just take anyone you know. These requirements are:

1. You must be between 17 and 39 years old.

2. You must be a citizen of the United States of America, or legal permanent resident.

3. You must have a high school diploma or have a GED with at least 15 college credits.

And even more important — you may NOT have a criminal record! That means you may not get arrested for _anything._ Getting arrested may ruin your chances of ever joining the Air Force or any of the United States Armed Forces.

Becoming a Pilot

The first step to becoming a pilot is becoming an OFFICER.

This means you have to go to college for 4 years and get a "BACHELOR'S DEGREE". In college you should study science, physics, aviation, or engineering. You will be flying planes after all, and you should know something about them before you fly them.

There are three ways to become an officer:

1. You can become an AIR FORCE CADET.

     a. To become an Air Force Cadet you must write to your Senator and ask him to nominate you. Thousands of kids each year apply, so if you want to be chosen you must have EXCEPTIONAL grades in school!

2. You can go to college first, on your own. Then when you have a bachelor's degree you can apply to the Air Force OFFICER'S TRAINING SCHOOL.

3. AFROTC: One of the best ways to become an Air Force pilot is to join the Air Force Reserve Officers Training Corps. When you do this, the Air Force helps you through college and even pays some of your tuition! Additionally you are committed to joining the Air Force once you graduate college. During your college studies you are already a CADET.

You Gotta go to College Kids!

Air Force Officer Ranks

Pay grade	O-1	O-2	O-3	O-4	O-5	O-6	O-7	O-8	O-9	O-10	Special[1]
Insignia											
Title	Second Lieutenant	First Lieutenant	Captain	Major	Lieutenant Colonel	Colonel	Brigadier General	Major General	Lieutenant General	General	General of the Air Force
Abbreviation[2]	2d Lt	1st Lt	Capt	Maj	Lt Col	Col	Brig Gen	Maj Gen	Lt Gen	Gen	GAF
NATO Code	OF-1		OF-2	OF-3	OF-4	OF-5	OF-6	OF-7	OF-8	OF-9	OF-10

[1] Awarded during periods of a declared war.

[2] No periods are used in actual grade abbreviation.

Pilot Training School

Once you have completed Officer Training School, you finally get to learn how to fly in Pilot Training School. In Pilot Training School you will learn the basics of flight, training usually starts with the T-6 Texan II trainer aircraft:

T-6 Texan II

Pilot training school is very hard work and has many phases and tests along the way. Additionally with your training as a pilot you will continue your academic training. You NEVER stop learning! Once you have completed all phases of pilot training, you graduate from the USAF Pilot Training Program and are finally awarded your pilot's Wings!

Did you think only boys can be pilots?   Think again — there are a lot of girl pilots in the Air Force!

F-15 Eagle female pilots from the 3rd Wing at Elmendorf Air Force Base,Alaska.

Air Combat

Once you have completed your training as a pilot, your MISSION begins. Your mission as a fighter pilot is to maintain "AIR SUPERIORITY".

Air Superiority = AIR COMBAT

That means you OWN THE SKY.

You must control everyone and <u>everything</u> that comes into your AIRSPACE, if they are an enemy aircraft — you shoot them down!

Sometimes, if the other pilot is lucky, you just escort them out of your airspace.

An F-22 Raptor escorts a Russian TU-95 Bear bomber out of United States Airspace

The 6 O' clock position

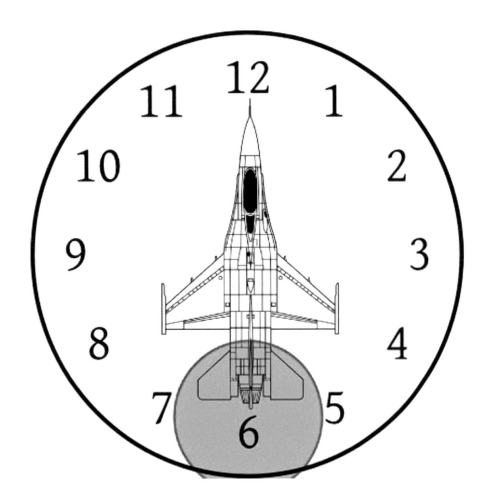

You may hear pilots say "Air Combat Maneuvering".
Another word for that is "DOGFIGHTING".
In the old days, (which is World War One and World War Two), when two fighter pilots engaged in air combat, they would circle around each other and "try to get the other's tail". This circling looked like two dogs when they fight, so the pilots started to call Air Combat DOGFIGHTING! Another thing you may here pilot's say is "I got his SIX". This means he got behind the other pilot — it's from the 6 o'clock position on a clock. Getting behind the enemy pilot is one of the main tactics to winning a DOGFIGHT. Most air combat maneuvering is done just to get into this position to shoot an enemy pilot down.

Two F-15 pilots during a training exercise. The rear pilot is in the perfect position --6 O'clock-- to score a kill!

Keep in mind, back then the pilots did not have high-tech air to air missiles, but only MACHINE GUNS, and very slow "BIPLANES", So they had to get really close to the other aircraft to shoot it down.

Fighter pilots try to get behind each other to fire their cannons

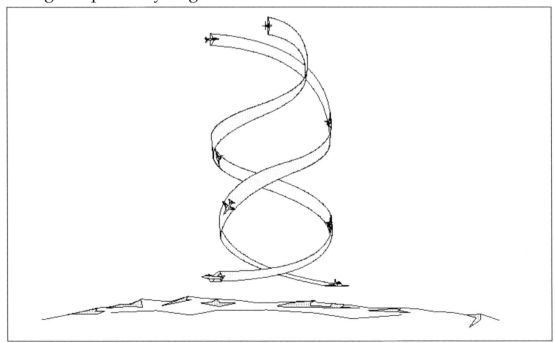

Air Combat is three dimensional!

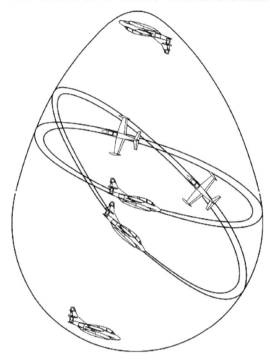

Besides circling and turning, a pilot must climb and dive his aircraft in order to try to get behind the other pilot and shoot him down.

It' all about WHO sees WHO first!

If you ever get in trouble, or an enemy pilot "gets your six", you will have to
EJECT!

An F-16 pilot ejects at an Airshow at Mt.Home AFB in Idaho in 2003

Even with the awesome high-tech air to air missiles we have nowadays, fighter aircraft still have cannons. In the picture below we can see the cannon's aperture right next to the pilot. It's that hole with vents that makes this F-16 look like a shark. Behind that hole is an M61 VULCAN CANNON.

A closer look at the M61 Vulcan Cannon in the F-16

The M61 Vulcan has six barrels and fires a 20mm projectile or bullet at 6,000 rounds per minute!

The M61 Vulcan cannon mounted in an F-15 Eagle

The M61 Vulcan Cannon on the ground

A cannon kill

A MIG-17 getting shot down by an F-105D over Vietnam in 1967.
The orange circles in the left of the picture are the pilot's GUNSIGHT.

Besides Vulcan cannons, modern fighter aircraft use AIR TO AIR MISSILES to shoot down an enemy fighter. This makes air combat much different today. Nowadays it is not only about getting behind the enemy aircraft for a better firing position, but it is also about *who sees who first!*

One of the very first air to air missiles, the AIM-9 SIDEWINDER

The Sidewinder is a heat-seeking missile, which means it locks on to the heat of the enemy aircraft's engine. Then it follows this heat all the way to the target — the enemy aircraft!

The heat seeking head of the Sidewinder

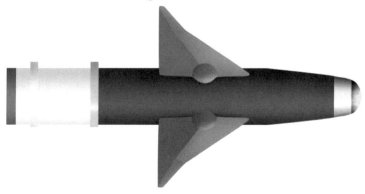

An AIM-9 Sidewinder destroys an F6F drone aircraft

An AIM-9 Sidewinder shoots down a QF4 drone

If an enemy fighter plane fires a heat seeking missile at you, you will have to take EVASIVE ACTION. One way to EVADE an enemy heat seeking missile is to fire off some FLARES. Flares burn very hotly, and distract the enemy missile away from your aircraft's hot engine and exhaust gas. Hopefully the enemy missile will follow the flares instead of you!

An F-15 Eagle takes evasive action by firing off some FLARES

If the flares work, the enemy missile will follow them, instead of you!

The AIM-7 Sparrow is a radar guided air to air missile.

An F-15C fires an AIM-7 Sparrow

The newer and better version of the AIM-7 Sparrow is called the   AIM-120 "AMRAAM", which stands for Advanced Medium Range Air to Air Missile. It has an active radar on board, so the pilot does not have to follow it after he fires it. This is called "FIRE AND FORGET". This way the pilot can fire a missile at an enemy aircraft and immediately turn around, or maneuver into position to attack another enemy aircraft.

This is what modern Air Combat Maneuvering <u>really</u> looks like today:

An F-16, shoots down a practice drone with an AIM-120 AMRAAM

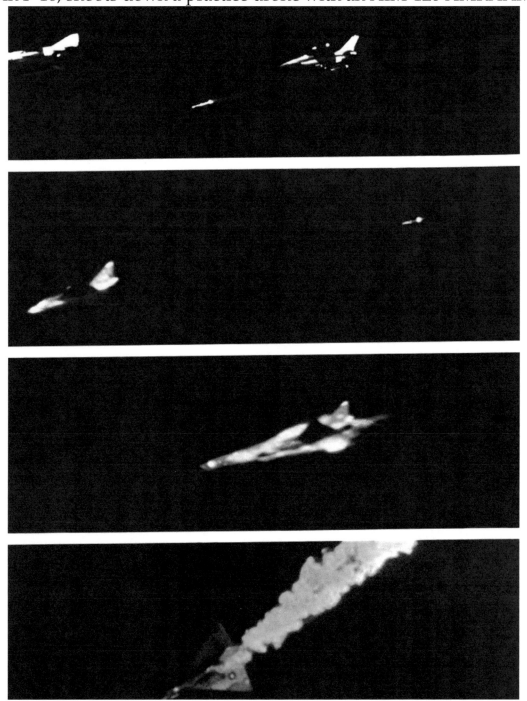

The main air superiority fighter of the USAF today is the F-15 Eagle

The F-15 is being replaced by the all new F-22 Raptor. It is the newest most advanced air superiority fighter of the United States Air Force.

The F-15 is one of the only aircraft in the world that can break the sound barrier going straight up, it is even faster than the space shuttle during launch!

Ground Support

After the Air Force achieves AIR SUPERIORITY, it can concentrate on GROUND SUPPORT, which often means GROUND ATTACK. This means the Air Force supports our soldiers and troops on the ground by:

Attacking enemy installations behind the lines

Destroying enemy tanks with AIR TO GROUND MISSILES

The A-10 Warthog launches an AGM-65 Maverick

The AGM-65 Maverick destroys a tank

Iraqi T54A destroyed during operation Desert Storm in 1990

Attacking ground positions with the AC-130 Spectre Gunship

Bombing enemy ground positions with guided bombs

Destroying enemy bunkers with "Bunker Buster" Bombs

The USAF Fleet

Fighters

F-15 Eagle

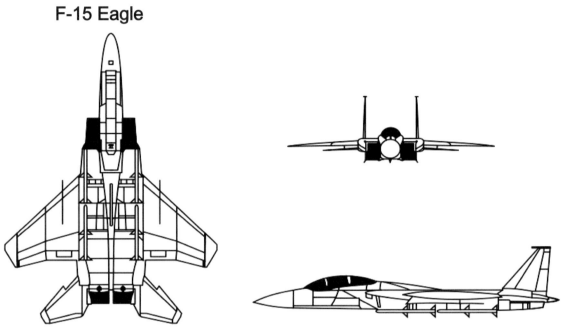

Crew: 1: pilot
Length: 63 ft 9 in (19.43 m)
Wingspan: 42 ft 10 in (13.05 m)
Height: 18 ft 6 in (5.63 m)
Wing area: 608 ft² (56.5 m²)
Empty weight: 28,000 lb (12,700 kg)
Powerplant: 2 × Pratt & Whitney F100-100 or −220 afterburningturbofans
Dry thrust: 14,590 lbf(64.9 kN) each
Thrust with afterburner: 23,770 lbf for −220(105.7 kN for −220) each
Maximum speed:
High altitude: Mach 2.5+ (1,650+ mph, 2,665+ km/h)
Low altitude: Mach 1.2 (900 mph, 1,450 km/h)
Combat radius: 1,061 nmi (1,222 mi, 1,967 km) for interdiction mission
Service ceiling: 65,000 ft (20,000 m)
Rate of climb: >50,000 ft/min (254 m/s)
Wing loading: 73.1 lb/ft² (358 kg/m²)
Thrust/weight: 1.07 (−220)
Maximum design g-load: 9 g
Guns: 1× 20 mm (0.787 in) M61A1 Vulcan 6-barreled Gatling cannon, 940 rounds

Missiles:
4× AIM-7 Sparrow
4× AIM-9 Sidewinder
8× AIM-120 AMRAAM

The F-15 Eagle is the main Air Superiority fighter of the United States Air Force. It's main mission is to go out and intercept enemy fighter aircraft and destroy them. It was built to rule the skies!

It is among the most successful modern fighters, with over 100 aerial combat victories. The newer version of the F-15 is the F15E "STRIKE EAGLE". It is a two seater version with extra drop tanks underneath the wings. This enables the F-15 to fly longer and deeper into enemy territory to make the strike!

F-15 refueling

F-15D Cockpit

The F-15 is so successful even other countries buy it for their Air Forces:

A British RAF F-15 over Iraq

An Israeli F-15 during training in Nevada

F-16 Falcon

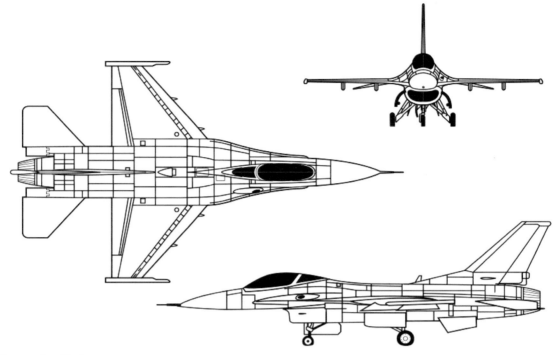

Crew: 1 pilot
Length: 49 ft 5 in (15.06 m)
Wingspan: 32 ft 8 in (9.96 m)
Height: 16 ft (4.88 m)
Empty weight: 18,900 lb (8,570 kg)
Powerplant: 1 × F110-GE-100 afterburning turbofan
Dry thrust: 17,155 lbf (76.3 kN)
Thrust with afterburner: 28,600 lbf (127 kN)
Maximum speed:
At sea level: Mach 1.2 (915 mph, 1,470 km/h)
At altitude: Mach 2 (1,320 mph, 2,120 km/h) clean configuration
Thrust/weight: 1.095
Guns: 1× 20 mm (0.787 in) M61A1 Vulcan 6-barrel Gatling cannon, 511 rounds
Missiles and Rockets: 2× AIM-7 Sparrow, 6× AIM-9 Sidewinder, 6× AIM-120 AMRAAM

The F-16 is the smallest and lightest fighter aircraft in the USAF fleet. It was developed as part of the Light Weight Fighter (LWF) program.

F-16

Length	49.7 ft
Span	31 ft
Wing Area	300 ft²
Internal Fuel	7,162 lb

F-35 CTOL

Length	51.1 ft
Span	35 ft
Wing Area	460 ft²
Internal Fuel	18,073 lb

F-22

Length	62.1 ft
Span	44.5 ft
Wing Area	840 ft²

After the Vietnam war, the Air Force recognized the need for a small aircraft that could out maneuver any other enemy aircraft and win a dogfight. It was designed by scientists to turn and climb better than any other aircraft in air combat. It has a power to weight ratio of 1.095, that means its jet engine puts out more thrust than the actual weight of the aircraft. This enables the F-16 to climb vertically like a rocket!

An F-16 in a vertical climb

A fully loaded F-16 of the Air National Guard

An F-16 fires defensive flares

An F-16 pilot with night vision goggles on

F-22 Raptor

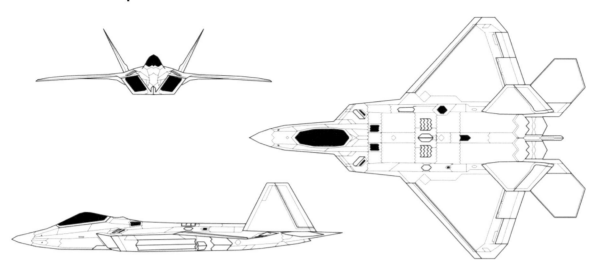

Crew: 1
Length: 62 ft 1 in (18.92 m)
Wingspan: 44 ft 6 in (13.56 m)
Height: 16 ft 8 in (5.08 m)
Powerplant: 2 × Pratt & Whitney F119-PW-100 pitch thrust vectoring turbofans:
Dry thrust: 26,000 lb (116 kN) each
Thrust with afterburner: 35,000+ lb (156+ kN) each
Maximum speed:
At altitude: Mach 2.25 (1,500 mph, 2,410 km/h)
Supercruise: Mach 1.82 (1,220 mph, 1,960 km/h)
Service ceiling: >65,000 ft (20,000 m)
Thrust/weight: 1.08
Guns: 1× 20 mm (0.787 in) M61A2 Vulcan 6-barrel Gatling cannon in right wing root, 480 rounds.
Air to air Missiles: 6× AIM-120 AMRAAM, 2× AIM-9 Sidewinder

The F-22 is the biggest fighter in the USAF fleet. It is also the first fighter that can "SUPERCRUISE". That means it can fly faster than the speed of sound without using its afterburners. This makes the F-22 fly faster and farther, without burning as much fuel, a very important capability for a fighter aircraft!

An F-22 accelerating with full afterburner. The afterburner adds extra thrust for maneuvering. Other aircraft must use the afterburner to achieve supersonic flight.

Unlike other aircraft, the F-22 carries all of its weapons internally in its weapons bay, that is on the inside. You will never see the rockets and missiles of the F-22. This is done not only to streamline the aircraft and make it faster, but to make it "stealthier" and harder to see by enemy radar.

An F-22 with its weapons bay doors open

Water vapor forms on the wings of an F-22

This can happen when you pull high G's and there is a lot of humidity or water in the air. That means turning really sharp so that the air literally "rips" over your wings and separates the water from the air! What is really happening is that the low pressure area above the wings is enabling the water in the air to come out, and separate itself from the air, a lot like boiling water to make steam.

F-35 Lightning II

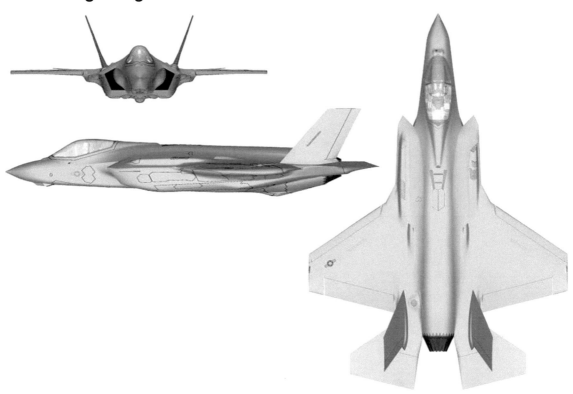

Crew: 1
Length: 50.5 ft (15.67 m)
Wingspan: 35 ft (10.7 m)
Height: 14.2 ft (4.33 m)
Powerplant: 1 × Pratt & Whitney F135 afterburning turbofan
Dry thrust: 28,000 lbf (125 kN)
Thrust with afterburner: 43,000 lbf (191 kN)
Maximum speed: Mach 1.6+ (1,200 mph, 1,930 km/h)
Guns: 1 × General Dynamics 25 mm (0.984 in) GAU-22/A 4-barrel Gatling gun, internally mounted with 180 rounds.
Air-to-air missiles: AIM-120 AMRAAM, AIM-9X Sidewinder, Long Range Anti-Ship Missile (LRASM)

The F-35 Lightning II is the newest addition to the Air force fleet. It is called a "Joint Strike Fighter" or JSF. It was designed for all of the armed forces, mainly the Air Force, Navy, and Marines. It can perform many missions and in the Marines version it can even start and land vertically — like a helicopter!

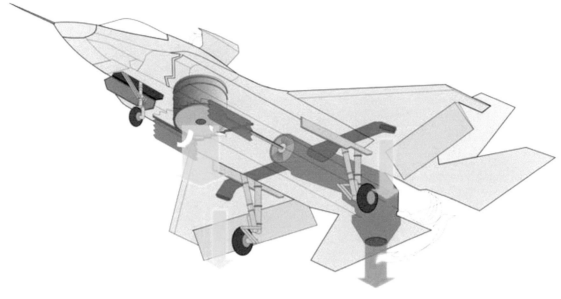

The F-35 landing vertically on an aircraft carrier

The F-35 taking off from an aircraft carrier.
You can see its rear nozzle pointing downward to increase lift:

An F-35 flying upside down – showing off its weapons

The F-35 has the most advanced weapons system than any other fighter in the USAF fleet. This includes the new helmet mounted display system:

■ Active Matrix Liquid Crystal Display image display

■ Sensor fusion

■ Binocular 40 degree by degree field-of-view

■ Integrated day and night camera

■ Ejection Safe to 600 knots equivalent air speed

This system enables the pilot to control his weapons without looking down at the control panel in the cockpit. He can find targets and enemy planes and fire his missiles at them without even maneuvering his aircraft. Everything is displayed inside his helmet! This gives the pilot the competitive edge he needs in air combat.

Ground Attack Aircraft

A-10 Thunderbolt II " Warthog"

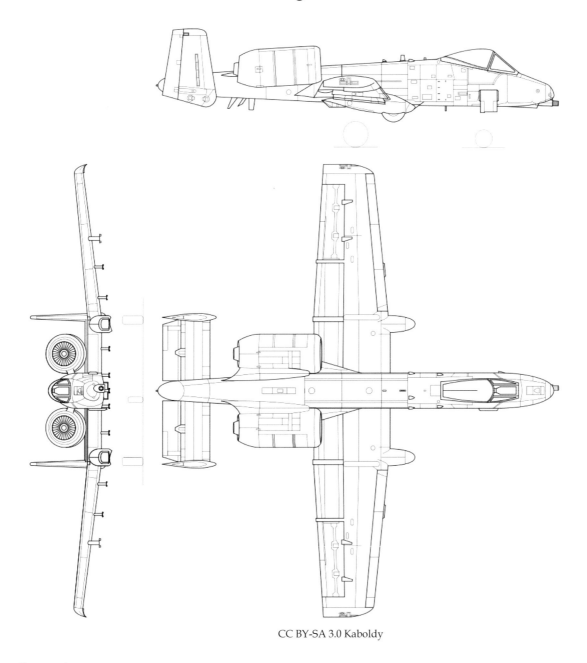

Crew: 1
Length: 53 ft 4 in (16.26 m)
Wingspan: 57 ft 6 in (17.53 m)
Height: 14 ft 8 in (4.47 m)
Empty weight: 24,959 lb (11,321 kg)
Powerplant: 2 × General Electric TF34-GE-100A turbofans

Maximum speed: 381 knots (439 mph, 706 km/h) at sea level, clean
Cruise speed: 300 knots (340 mph, 560 km/h)
Service ceiling: 45,000 ft (13,700 m)
Thrust/weight: 0.36
Guns: 1× 30 mm (1.18 in) GAU-8/A Avenger Gatling cannon with 1,174 rounds (Capacity 1,350)
Rockets:
4× LAU-61/LAU-68 rocket pods (each with 19× / 7× Hydra 70 mm rockets, respectively)
4× LAU-5003 rocket pods (each with 19× CRV7 70 mm rockets)
6× LAU-10 rocket pods (each with 4× 127 mm (5.0 in) Zuni rockets
Missiles:
2× AIM-9 Sidewinders air-to-air missiles for self-defense
6× AGM-65 Maverick air-to-surface missiles

When you destroy an enemy tank or armor, the "kill" is painted on the side of your aircraft. How many Tanks has this aircraft "killed"? How many radars?

The A-10 Thunderbolt in action over Afghanistan

The A-10 is one of the only aircraft which was built entirely around a cannon!

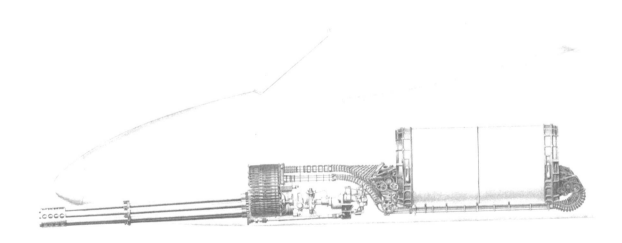

Front view of the 30 mm GAU-8/A Avenger Gatling cannon

The A-10's cannon is bigger than a car!

A-10 Thunderbolt firing its 30mm cannon

Water Vapor above the wings of an A-10 during a high G turn

The A-10's engines are above and behind the wings to make it harder for enemy heat seeking missiles to detect them and home in on them.

A-10 Thunderbolt cockpit. The square piece of glass in the middle is called a "Heads Up Display" or HUD. It is also the gunsight for the 30mm cannon.

An A-10 showing a full payload

Cutaway view of the A-10

A-10 INBOARD PROFILE

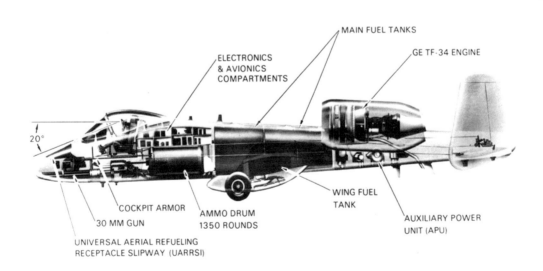

AC-130 Spectre

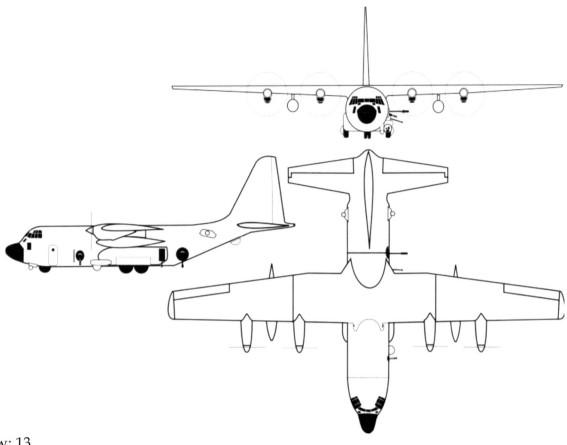

Crew: 13
Length: 97 ft 9 in (29.8 m)
Wingspan: 132 ft 7 in (40.4 m)
Height: 38 ft 6 in (11.7 m)
Max. takeoff weight: 155,000 lb (69,750 kg)
Powerplant: 4 × Allison T56-A-15 turboprops, 4,910 shp (3,700 kW) each

Armament:
AC-130A Project Gunship II
4× 7.62 mm GAU-2/A miniguns
4× 20 mm (0.787 in) M61 Vulcan 6-barrel Gatling cannon
AC-130A Surprise Package, Pave Pronto, AC-130E Pave Spectre
2× 7.62 mm GAU-2/A miniguns
2× 20 mm M61 Vulcan cannon
2× 40 mm (1.58 in) L/60 Bofors cannon

'Gunslinger' weapons system with launch tube for AGM-176 Griffin missiles and/or GBU-44/B
Viper Strike munitions (10 round magazines)
Wing mounted, AGM-114 Hellfire missiles, GBU-39 Small Diameter Bombs (SDBs) and/or
GBU-53/B SDB IIs

AC-130 Spectre firing defensive flares

When we use an aircraft as a PLATFORM for guns, cannons and weapons, we call it a "GUNSHIP", even though it is an airplane.   The Lockheed AC-130 Spectre (sometimes called "Spooky") is the premier gunship of the United States with a wide range of weapons which it uses for GROUND ATTACK missions.

The AC-130 even has a 105mm howitzer cannon onboard!

Inside the control room: sensor displays of the AC-130 Spooky Gunship

The 20mm M61 Vulcan cannons

Reconnaissance

Reconnaisance aircraft or "SPY PLANES" are designed to fly high and fast over enemy territory to take high resolution photos. These photos are then used to see where the enemy installations are. Reconnaissance is just a fancy word for SPY.

The pilots in reconnaissance aircraft fly so high that they must wear the same suits as astronauts to survive at high altitude.

U-2 Dragon Lady

Crew: One
Length: 63 ft (19.2 m)
Wingspan: 103 ft (31.4 m)
Height: 16 ft (4.88 m)
Powerplant: 1 × General Electric F118-101 turbofan, 19,000lbf (85 kN)
Performance
Maximum speed: 434 knots (Mach 0.67, 500 mph, 805 km/h)
Cruise speed: 373 knots (Mach 0.56, 429 mph, 690 km/h)
Stall speed: 80-90 mph near ground
Range: 5,566 nmi (6,405mi, 10,300 km)
Service ceiling: 70,000+ ft (21,300+ m)
lift-to-drag: 23:1
Flight endurance: 12 hours

The U-2 Dragon Lady is still in service with the United States Air Force today. When satellite photos are not enough, a spy plane must fill the gap.

SR-71 Blackbird

One of the most awesome aircraft in the USAF fleet was the SR-71.   The SR-71 was designed to fly high and fast over enemy territory. The SR-71 could fly "MACH 3", that means it flew three times faster than the speed of sound. It was so fast that enemy anti-aircraft missiles couldn't even catch it!

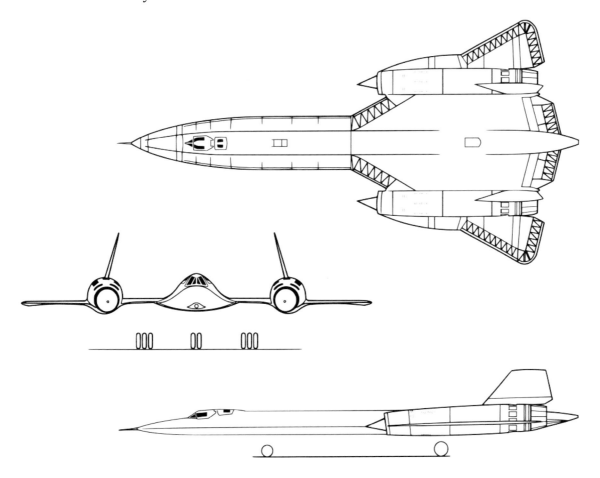

Crew: 2 (Pilot and Reconnaissance Systems Officer)
Length: 107 ft 5 in (32.74m)
Wingspan: 55 ft 7 in (16.94m)
Height: 18 ft 6 in (5.64m)
Powerplant: 2 × Pratt & Whitney J58-1 continuous-bleed afterburning turbojets, 34,000 lbf(151kN) each
Maximum speed: Mach 3.3 (2,200+ mph, 3,540+ km/h, 1,910+ knots) at 80,000ft (24,000m)
Range: 2,900nmi (5,400km)
Service ceiling: 85,000 ft (25,900 m)
Rate of climb: 11820 ft/m (60m/s)
Thrust/weight: 0.44

SR-71 Blackbird two seater version

The SR-71 Blackbird has twin rudders, also called vertical stabilizers. They are canted inwards to make the Blackbird less susceptible to side winds.

The pilots of the U-2 and SR-71 fly so high that they can actually see the curvature of the earth!

Bombers

B-1B Lancer

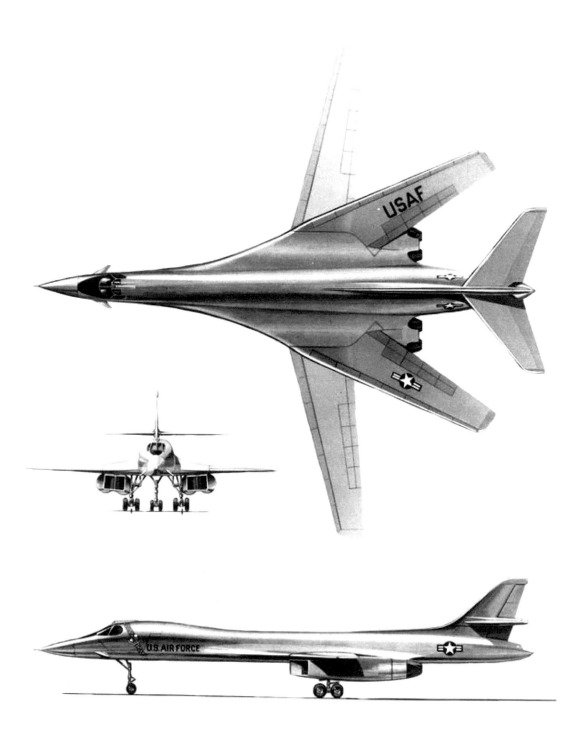

Crew: four (aircraft commander, copilot, offensive systems officer and defensive systems officer)

Length: 146 ft (44.5 m)

Wingspan:

Extended: 137 ft (41.8 m)

Swept: 79 ft (24 m))

Height: 34 ft (10.4 m)

Powerplant: 4 × General Electric F101-GE-102 augmented turbofans

Range: 6,478 nmi (7,456 mi (11,999 km))

Combat radius: 2,993 nmi (3,445 mi (5,544 km))

Service ceiling: 60,000 ft (18,000 m)

Bombs:

84× Mk-82 Air inflatable retarder (AIR) general purpose (GP) bombs

81× Mk-82 low drag general purpose (LDGP) bombs[168]

84× Mk-62 Quickstrike sea mines

24× Mk-84 general purpose bombs

24× Mk-65 naval mines

30× CBU-87/89/CBU-97 Cluster Bomb Units (CBU)

24× GBU-31 JDAM GPS guided bombs (Mk-84 GP or BLU-109 warhead)

15× GBU-38 JDAM GPS guided bombs (Mk-82 GP warhead)

48x GBU-54 Laser JDAM (using rotary launcher mounted multiple ejector racks)

24× AGM-154 Joint Standoff Weapon (JSOW)

The B-1B Lancer has "swing wings", that means it can move its wings forwards or backwards in order to make it fly better. When the pilot wants to fly fast, he swings the wings backwards. When he wants to take off or land, he swings the wings forwards or outwards, this is better for slow speeds and helps him land on shorter runways.

B-1B with wings forward

B-1B with wings swept backward

B-2 Spirit

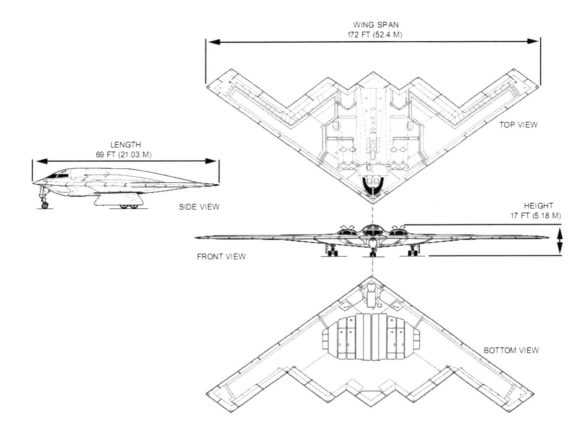

Crew: 2: pilot and commander (co-pilot)
Length: 69 ft (21.0 m)
Wingspan: 172 ft (52.4 m)
Height: 17 ft (5.18 m)
Max. takeoff weight: 376,000 lb (170,600 kg)
Powerplant: 4 × General Electric F118-GE-100 non-afterburning turbofans, 17,300 lbf (77 kN)
each
Maximum speed: Mach 0.95 (550 knots, 630 mph, 1,010 km/h) at 40,000 ft altitude / Mach
0.95 at sea level
Range: 6,000 nmi (11,100 km (6,900 mi))
Service ceiling: 50,000 ft (15,200 m)
Armament:
2 internal bays for 50,000 lb (23,000 kg) of ordnance and payload[61]
80× 500 lb class bombs (Mk-82, GBU-38) mounted on Bomb Rack Assembly (BRA)
36× 750 lb CBU class bombs on BRA
16× 2,000 lb class bombs (Mk-84, GBU-31) mounted on Rotary Launcher Assembly (RLA)
16× B61 or B83 nuclear bombs on RLA (strategic mission)

The B-2 Spirit is a STEALTH BOMBER. The shape of the airframe, and materials it is made out of, make it invisible to enemy radar. It is used to fly high and deep into enemy territory and deliver it's payload – bombs! It also has the distinct honor of being the most expensive aircraft in the world. It cost 2.4 billion dollars to produce! The B-2 also has no tail, no rudder, no elevator, no horizontal stabilizer and no vertical stabilizer. It's all wing – that's why it's also called a "flying wing".

B-2 Spirit stealth bomber

B-2 Spirit delivering its payload

B-52 Stratofortress

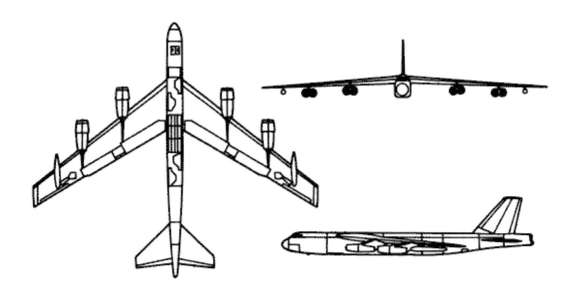

Crew: 5 (pilot, copilot, Weapon Systems Officer, navigator, Electronic Warfare Officer, and tail gunner until the removal of the tail gun in 1991)
Length: 159ft, 4 in (48.5   m)
Wingspan: 185ft, 0in (56.4   m)
Height: 40ft, 8in (12.4   m)
Wing area: 4,000 square feet (370 m²)
Max. takeoff weight: 488,000 lb (220,000 kg)
Powerplant: 8 × Pratt & Whitney TF33-P-3/103 turbofans, 17,000 lbf (76 kN) each
Maximum speed: 560 kt (650 mph, 1,047 km/h)
Combat radius: 4,480 mi (3,890 nmi, 7,210 km)
Bombs: Approximately 70,000 lb (31,500 kg) mixed ordnance; bombs, mines, missiles, in various configurations

The B-52 is the oldest aircraft in the Air Force fleet, it has been flying since the 1950's and it is still flying today. It can deliver 70,000 pounds of bombs!

Cargo Aircraft / Airlifters

Cargo aircraft are used to support the troops on the ground by delivering supplies, weapons, and more soldiers. Not only can they be used for wartime missions, but cargo aircraft can also be used for humanitarian missions, like delivering food or rescuing people after hurricane or storm. Cargo aircraft are also called "AIRLIFTERS".

C-5 Galaxy

The C-5 Galaxy is the biggest aircraft in the USAF fleet, and one of the largest military aircraft in the world.

Crew: 7 typical (aircraft commander, pilot, two flight engineers, three loadmasters)
Payload: 270,000 lb (122,470 kg)
Length: 247 ft 1 in (75.31 m)

Wingspan: 222 ft 9 in (67.89 m)
Height: 65 ft 1 in (19.84 m)
Max. takeoff weight: 840,000 lb (381,000 kg)
Powerplant: 4 × General Electric TF39-GE-1C high-bypass turbofan, 43,000 lbf (190 kN) each
Maximum speed: Mach 0.79 (503 kn, 579 mph, 932 km/h)
Takeoff roll: 8,400 ft (2,600 m)
Landing roll: 3,600 ft (1,100 m)

The C-5 Galaxy is loaded from the front or the rear

C-17 Globemaster III

Built in Long Beach California, the C-17 is one of the most versatile airlifters in the world. Because of its engine and wing configuration, it is able to take off and land on extremely short runways for such a large aircraft.

Crew: 3: 2 pilots, 1 loadmaster
Capacity:
102 paratroopers or
134 troops with palletized and sidewall seats or
54 troops with sidewall seats (allows 13 cargo pallets) only or
36 litter and 54 ambulatory patients and medical attendants or
Cargo, such as an M1 Abrams tank, three Strykers, or six M1117 Armored Security Vehicles
Payload: 170,900 lb (77,519 kg) of cargo distributed at max over 18 463L master pallets or a mix of palletized cargo and vehicles
Length: 174 ft (53 m)
Wingspan: 169.8 ft (51.75 m)
Height: 55.1 ft (16.8 m)
Max. takeoff weight: 585,000 lb (265,350 kg)
Powerplant: 4 × Pratt & Whitney F117-PW-100 turbofans, 40,440 lbf (180 kN) each

Thirteen C-17 Globemaster III 's fly over the Blue Ridge Mountains in Virginia during low level tactical training

Acknowledgements

At this point I would like to thank my expert contributors, I am forever grateful to them. Not only have they enabled me to make one of the finest books on the subject and provide something of value, but they have also enabled me to make a book which I will be proud and confident to give to any child and say, "here you go kid, from our men and women of the USAF to you!"

I hope you enjoyed this book and are on your way to becoming an Air Force pilot now! Thank you for buying and reading this book and trusting me to offer something of value.

If you liked this book you may like my others at
www.thekidsbooks.blogspot.com .

THE END

GET NAVY SEALS FOR KIDS
For FREE
Just type this into your browser:

https://goo.gl/SQS68M

You must type it EXACTLY like above,

Enjoy your free Ebook!

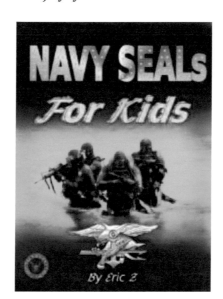

The KIDS BOOKS

www.thekidsbooks.blogspot.com

Visit ME!
TheKidsBooks.Blogspot.com

Made in United States
Troutdale, OR
02/19/2024

17815825R00055